Dedication

To those involved in some of the disasters that have come to change the way we think about such events.

Sept 11 2001   World Trade Center Collapse

July 6 1988   Piper Alpha Rig Disaster

Dec 21 1988   Pan Am Flight 103. Lockerbie

Mar 6 1987   Herald of Free Enterprise Capsize

Jan 28 1986   Challenger Space Shuttle Disaster

Oct 5 1999   Ladbroke Grove Rail Crash

Apr 15 1989   Hillsborough Disaster

July 7 2005   The London '7/7' bombings

Mar 8 2014   Malaysian Airlines Flight MH370

Dec 2 1984   Bhopal

Dec 11 2005   Buncefield Oil Terminal Explosion

Apr 24 2013   Bangladesh Factory Collapse

Apr 26 1986   Chernobyl Nuclear Reactor Explosion

Apr 20 2010   Deepwater Horizon Blowout

And since this list was made:

July 22 2014   Malaysian Airlines Flight MH17 missile strike

July 2014   Costa Concordia wreck removed to Genoa

July 2014   Ebola Virus outbreak in Sub-Saharan Africa

There will be more to come!

Copyright

Disclaimer

Whilst I have made every effort to ensure accuracy and that the text is up to date, I cannot accept legal liability for its contents. Specialist advice should always be sought, especially in legal matters!

Copyright

Hyperlinks

Hyperlinks are extensively used, particularly to many excellent UK Government publications which relate to emergency planning. These are prone to being changed and your forbearance is requested should this arise. In the printed version of this book it will be necessary to copy the hyperlinks and copy them into a search engine.

Purpose of this book.

Whilst there is much relevant authoritative literature available, there is a need for a basic primer publication aimed at the busy executive or practitioner to take them into the process of appreciating the need for and the practicalities of implementation of a DEMS.

This book endeavours to do just that!

Contents

Introduction

A brief history of disasters

The history of disaster is as old as mankind and it is a sad certainty that the bigger we get, the harder we seem to fall.

Some disasters find a special place in history, from Noah's flood to the Bhopal Disaster in India (in which a lethal cloud of toxic chemical killed and maimed many thousands of innocent, unprepared people). Most of us worldwide will have heard of the destruction of the World Trade Center in New York on September 11 2001 but everybody will have their own personal repository of some of the many disasters that have plagued us and will, it seems, inevitably continue to do so. Disasters are the stuff of media attention. Headlines broadcast them with almost gleeful delight no matter how much loss and suffering occur as a consequence of them. Some disasters are created by the media themselves or at least they have a major role in promulgating them. The News-International Phone Hacking Scandal is an excellent example! We look at media management later.

Man-made and natural disasters

It is useful to distinguish between the two in the sense that an angry nature, a so called 'Act of God' can be randomly inflicted upon us, sometimes without warning and completely unexpectedly. On the other hand, mankind has an almost uncanny ability to create his own disasters. We go to war, we neglect our infrastructure until our trains crash, our flood defences fail, our buildings fall down etc.

When nature acts to shake our world with earthquakes, hurricanes, tsunamis and volcanic eruptions we are helpless in preventing them but we are irresponsible if we have no measures in place to mitigate their effects. Too often, then many of us suffer hardship, loss and bereavement. Neatly summed up as the biblical 'Four horsemen of the Apocalypse' (Pestilence, War, Famine and Death).

Why some enterprises survive and others do not

On Sept 11 2001, some companies in the world Trade Center were destroyed with it. Some other companies continued to function, even on the same day of the disaster.

An office block was set on fire and partially destroyed because it was close to an oil terminal at a place called Buncefield, which blew up in an accident due to 'a whole host of safety related failures' (HSE Report)

Companies with premises there were denied access for some days and some of those companies failed as a result of the business interruption.

It is generally acknowledged that around 40% of businesses that suffer a major fire never restart. Of those that do survive, most fail within two years of the fire.

It is no accident that some recover and that some do not. Those that survive do so because they have some kind of contingency planning in place, that they have some idea of what to do if disaster strikes. There is a degree of preparedness and resilience and, vitally, there are management systems to give a structured response and a structured way forward in the aftermath. It is the purpose of this book to enable you, the manager or management team it is aimed at to implement and operate such a DEMS.

Some terminology

We need to know what we are talking about so we must think about how some crucial terms are defined. This is not a particularly straightforward matter because the words we use may mean different things to different people and organisations. The media are particularly loose in their use of words and have an innate tendency towards exaggeration. Concerns about the meaning of key terminology may cause conflict in defining and therefore creating policy and management systems.

There is no international clarity on terminology. In the U.K. we use the term 'Emergency Planning', in the U.S.A 'Crisis Management' is preferred. Communication is a key concept in every 'Major Incident' inquiry or investigation. It can be said that 50% of communication failures are attributable to people calling the same thing by different names and the other 50% are due to people calling different things by the same name.

You need to be able to classify an event in order to determine an appropriate response. An 'Incident' will have a different response to say a 'Catastrophe'.

Definitions matter for legal, insurance, managerial and policy reasons.

So with that caveat, here goes:

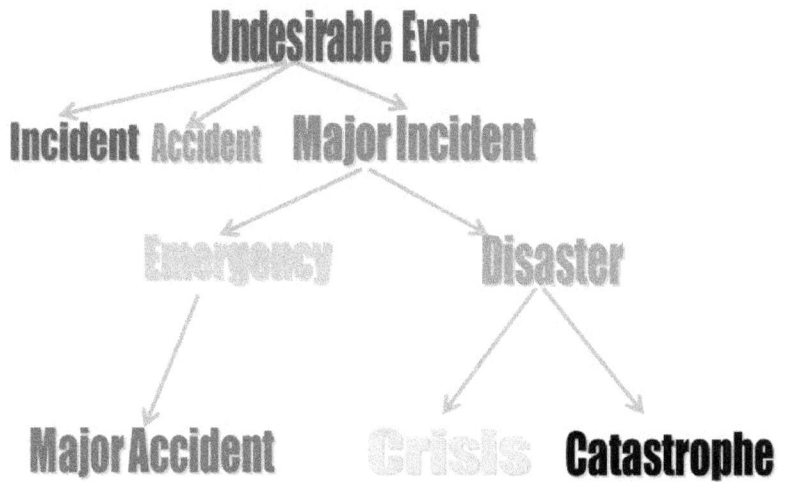

An 'undesirable event' is used as a header for:

incident – usually thought of as a 'damage only' accident;

accident – invariably meaning injury to persons;

emergency – a threat about to be realised;

disaster – the outcome of an unmanaged emergency, having consequences that threaten the survival of the organisation and maybe others that depend on it;

major incident and **major accident** have specific meanings for the emergency services and are taken as requiring a response beyond the normal service capability (for example an accident involving more than 50 serious casualties);

Crisis – an ongoing emergency which is difficult to resolve (such as an outbreak of pandemic 'flu or the Deepwater Horizon blowout);

Catastrophe – beyond disaster, when the existing emergency response is overwhelmed and there is no organised assistance for those in distress.

Threat – a hazard of sufficient severity to endanger an organisation if it should be realised. Note that only severe 'significant' hazards which may seriously harm the organisation are ranked as threats. A workplace accident would not be considered to be a threat unless it had such damaging implications that it would put the enterprise out of business or severely damage it. We shall look at threats and threat assessment when we consider the implementation of a DEMS.

There are many other important terms which we shall meet but the above will serve to start us off.

Chapter 1   The Need for a DEMS

In order to forsee and sometimes be able to prevent an emergency arising and then to mitigate the consequences of a potential disaster, a coordinated response is essential. We won't get away with it if we try to 'wing it' when the worst happens. This book is about how to put an effective DEMS in place.

Within any management system there are legal, moral and financial aspects and this is especially true of a DEMS.

The **moral** case for having an operational DEMS rests in that it could save your business from foundering, letting down your suppliers and your customers, the livelihood of your employees and even their lives and the lives of others. In all circumstances it will greatly reduce your physical and reputational losses and often enable you to come through it with your reputation actually enhanced!

The direct **financial** case is associated with loss prevention and loss mitigation as is also the case with Health, Safety and Environmental Management Systems, but there are indirect benefits also. Having a DEMS in place brings reduced insurance premiums, a gentler regime of inspection by the various regulators (Health & Safety Executive, Environment Agency, Fire Authority), evidence of Corporate Social Responsibility (CSR) (a requirement, especially for larger companies to satisfy the requirements of the Turnbull Report on CSR) and a more favourable image and reputation with the company's stakeholders.

The **legal** case is about compliance with national legislation, international codes of practice and conventions.

The Management of Health & Safety Regulations (UK) require organisations to have procedures for 'imminent and serious danger'

Regulation 8 relates to serious and imminent danger at work. Employers are required to establish appropriate procedures, nominate sufficient people to implement them and ensure that untrained staff are not allowed access to dangerous areas.

At its simplest, this may only require adequate procedures for fire and, possibly, bomb threats. However, the risk assessment should identify any other situations that may arise requiring employees to evacuate all or part of the workplace

The Control of Major Accident Hazards Regulations 1999 (UK) and also within the ILO (International Labour Organisation NATLEX) database.

There is a specific ILO code for major hazards

http://www.ilo.org/dyn/natlex/natlex_browse.home

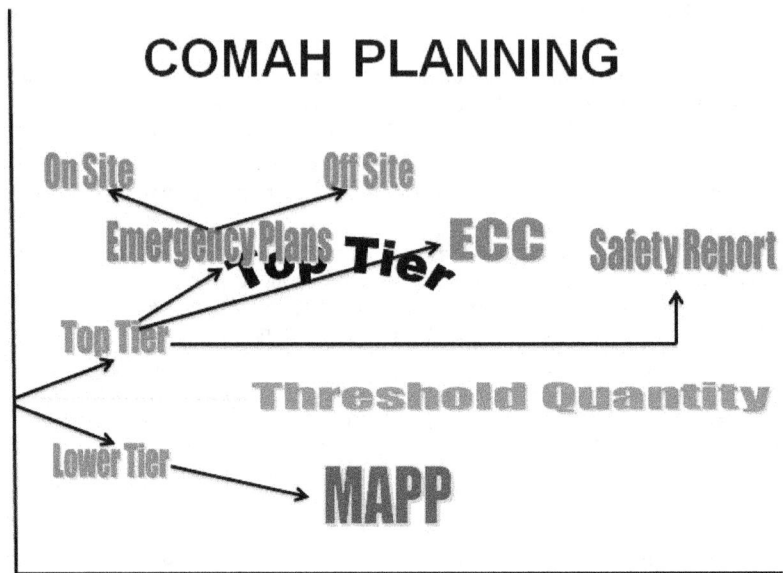

Major hazard sites are grouped into two tiers according to threshold quantities of hazardous substances they carry.

The lower tier calls for a Major Accident Prevention Plan.

The upper tier additionally requires specific on-site and off-site emergency plans to be in place as well as a site safety report and an emergency control centre.

Responsibilities of the CEO (Corporate Manslaughter and Corporate Homicide Act 2007). UK legislation places a duty on company executives who must bear the risk of personal prosecution if their employees or other persons, including emergency service personnel if they are grossly negligent.

Duties wrto fire precautions (Regulatory Reform (Fire safety) Order 2005)

Under UK law, duty is placed on the premises management of an enterprise to carry out fire risk assessments and have a fire management system in place. Fires are often disastrous for an organisation.

The main concern of this book is not about the relatively small number of comah sites which invariably have DEMS in place as a consequence of the regulations. Most enterprises worldwide are SMEs (Small to Medium) and the range is as wide as the entrepreneurial spirit of man.

Sources of advice and guidance.

International Labour Office (ILO)

http://www.ilo.org/oshenc/part-vi/disasters-natural-and-technological/item/364-disaster-preparedness

UK Cabinet Office.

https://www.gov.uk/government/organisations/cabinet-office

Federal Emergency Management Agency

http://www.fema.gov

Institute of Civil Protection & Emergency Management (ICPEM)

http://www.icpem.net

UK emergency Planning society

https://www.the-eps.org

Chapter 2   The Importance of Resilience

Resilience is perhaps the most vital aspect of a DEMS. The ability to respond quickly and flexibly to an emergency is paramount and for this to be achievable a number of things need to be in place. A useful illustration is the comparison between the Haitian earthquake of 12 Jan 2010, the Japanese earthquake and tsunami of 11 Mar 2011 and the impact of Hurricane Irene on the Eastern Seaboard of America in August of the same year.

I've quoted extensively and given hyperlinks to the very comprehensive coverage given by Wikipedia so that you can browse and consider what were the factors at play in these catastrophic events.

Case Studies – Disaster Responses

Haitian Earthquake

Six months after the quake as much as 98 percent of the rubble remained uncleared. An estimated 20 million cubic meters remained, making most of the capital impassable and thousands of bodies remained in the rubble. The number of people in relief camps of tents and tarps since the quake was 1.6 million, and almost no transitional housing had been built. Most of the camps had no electricity, running water, or sewage disposal, and the tents were beginning to fall apart. Crime in the camps was widespread, especially against women and girls. Between 23 major charities, US$1.1 billion had been collected for Haiti for relief efforts, but only two percent of the money had been released.

http://en.wikipedia.org/wiki/2010_Haiti_earthquake

Fukushima Tsunami

Japan's "rigid bureaucratic structures, reluctance to send bad news upwards, need to save face, weak development of policy alternatives, eagerness to preserve nuclear power's public acceptance, and politically fragile government, along with TEPCO's very hierarchical management culture, also contributed to the way the accident unfolded

http://en.wikipedia.org/wiki/Fukushima_Daiichi_nuclear_disaster

Hurricane Irene 28 Aug 2011

With Irene's projected path fixed over much of the United States East Coast, over 65 million people from the Carolinas to northern New England were estimated to be at risk. Due to the threat, state officials, as well as utilities, transportation facilities, ports, industries, oil refineries, and nuclear power plants, promptly prepared to activate emergency plans; residents in the areas stocked up on food supplies and worked to secure homes, vehicles and boats. States of emergency and hurricane warnings were declared for much of the East Coast.

Within a month of the storm 84 of 118 closed sections of state highway, and 28 of 34 bridges, had been reopened. The state had relied on assistance from National Guard units in eight other states, and highway workers lent to it by New Hampshire and Maine. "We'll do the work and we'll figure out how we're paying for it," said deputy state secretary of transportation Sue Minter, "but we're not waiting." Repair costs ultimately turned out to be $175–200 million, with most of it covered by federal disaster relief.

http://en.wikipedia.org/wiki/Hurricane_Irene

You should have recognised that the principal failings in response are basically down to cultural issues. Governmental structures in Haiti are notoriously weak so that rescue and recovery has largely been left to the United Nations and voluntary organisations. The Japanese culture is entirely opposite to this laissez faire attitude but suffers from an inbuilt fear of failure (loss of face) at both individual and corporate level vital information, thus inhibiting critical information flows.
The response to Hurricane Irene as a contrast shows how an emergency can be successfully managed and enhances the reputation of the nation and its president.
In the next chapter we look at the structures which need to be in place to enable an appropriately resilient emergency response.

Chapter 3   Emergency planning framework (UK Civil Contingencies Act 2004).

It is important for your enterprise that you understand the national framework for emergency response, consider its capability and how you would interact with it in the event of a serious emergency.

This is a responsibility of the Cabinet Office in the UK. You can get an overview by following the link:

https://www.gov.uk/emergency-response-and-recovery

Disaster management at national (and to some degree international) level is delegated to the 'blue light' emergency services with backup from the military if required. The Emergency Powers Act enables governments to declare a 'State of Emergency' which can suspend the normal rights of citizens (e.g. by applying a curfew) for a limited time while normality is restored.

Category one and Category two Responders.

The principal Category one are the police, fire and ambulance services. Police are given overall command with the fire service as 'technical support'.

Category two are bodies having a significant supporting role in an emergency situation. Local Authorities, the National Health Service, public utilities and transport companies fall into this category.

Response Levels.

In order to ensure a proportionate response, a series of response levels are defined.

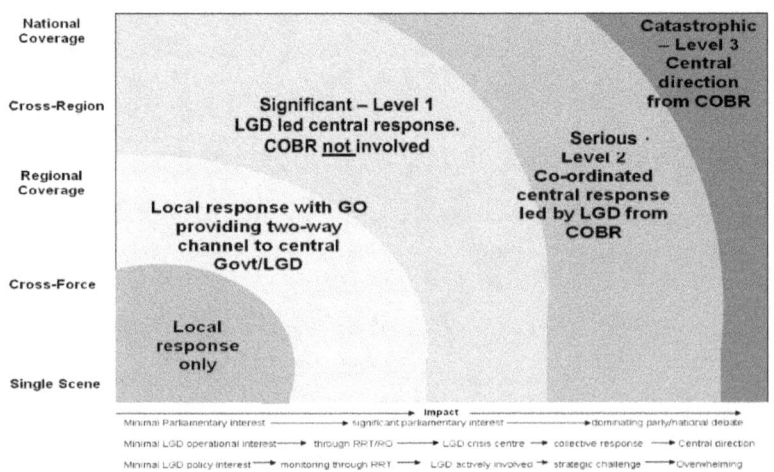

ANNEX B: LIKELY FORM OF CENTRAL GOVERNMENT ENGAGEMENT BASED ON THE IMPACT AND GEOGRAPHIC SPREAD OF AN EMERGENCY IN ENGLAND

Detailed downloadable guidance is available from the Cabinet Office 'Responding to Emergencies.'

(COBR is the Cabinet Office Briefing Room).

https://www.gov.uk/government/uploads/system/uploads/attachment_data/file/192425/CONOPs_in
cl_revised_chapter_24_Apr-13.pdf

Whilst the Emergency Planning Framework of the UK Government is referenced here, the structures follow the approach taken by the ILO: Code of Practice (duties of competent authorities).

Regional Resilience Forums

Emergency response is organised on a regional basis reflecting the structures of local authorities and agencies such as the Health & Safety Executive and the Environment Agency. Regional meetings are held so as to give a coherent approach by the various responders in planning for predictable emergencies (e.g. flooding).

Integrated Emergency Management

Making sure there is 'effective preparation' to manage emergencies (**pre-planning**).

Recognising the need for a **'division of labour'** between participants BUT there needs to be an overall **framework for co-ordination**.

The importance of **integrated emergency arrangements** – generic and specific (ie the 'what' and the 'how').

the need to appreciate that plans are about **RESPONSE** not CAUSATION. Plans need to cover an array of scenarios, under diverse natural, behavioural and social conditions.

Arrangements need to be **embedded** into everyday corporate life.

Integration of activities of different departments – establishment of **mou/protocols**.

Co-ordination with external agencies.

https://www.gov.uk/government/uploads/system/uploads/attachment_data/file/62228/recovery-emergency-management-guide.pdf

Chapter 4   Steps in implementation

Integrated Emergency Management (IEM) - an overview

Civil contingency planning
arrangements need to be
integrated both **within** and
between organisations.

- They should be an integral part of
  departmental and organisational planning.
- Organisations should work both
  individually and in collaboration with
  each other on key activities.

Five activities are key to an integrated approach

| Assess | Prevent | Prepare | Respond | Recover |

These activities all interact with each other - they are not separate stages

How a major incident is coordinated.

When a major incident arises it may involve the activation of 'Integrated Emergency Management', whereby the management of the major incident is then in the hand of the emergency services. This means your company's management has to work under the command and control of the emergency services. This does **not,** however mean that the police, fire, ambulance etc. will be 'running the business'; that is still a management responsibility. Importantly, your Crisis Management Team (CMT) will need to know where it fits into the command and control structure and its key function, namely to communicate instructions from the emergency services to staff and contractors.

Response levels to a major incident:

TEAM 1 (GOLD): Crisis Management Team - Strategic

TEAM 2 (SILVER): Emergency Management Team – Tactical

TEAM 3 (BRONZE): Incident Management Team – Operational

Although it important for you to understand how the emergency services respond and their command and control structures, you need to be proactive within your management as to the level of response and who takes command internally. The strength of this system is that the structure is in place to upgrade or downgrade the response according to the ongoing assessment of risk.

The critical stakeholders in any 'combined response'

Typical management of a major emergency. You should note the complexity of these arrangements and why an integrated response is essential.

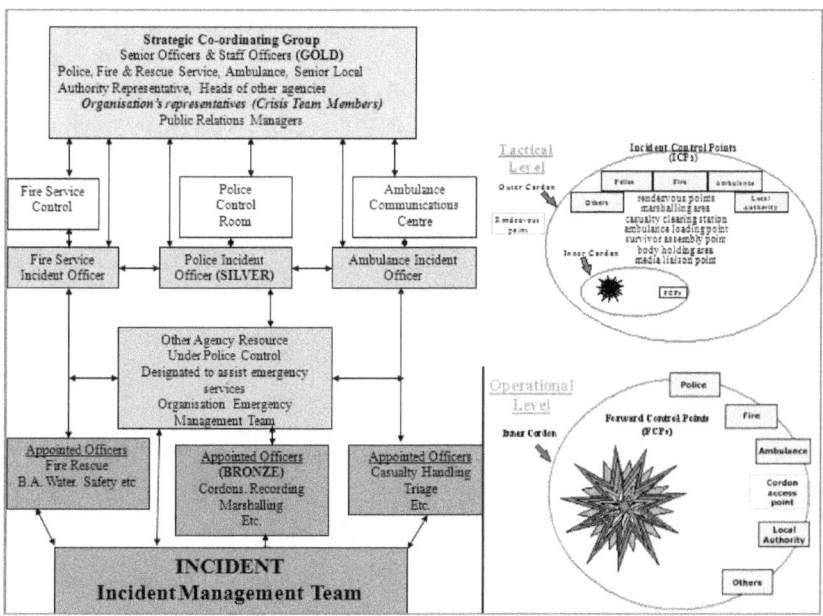

Case Study – the 7/7 Bombings

During the morning rush hour of 7th July 2005 a bus exploded outside one of London's biggest hotels. The emergency arrangements required the establishment of a number of cordons. The casualty clearing station and a temporary mortuary were set up in the hotel. In the midst of the horror that was unfolding before their eyes, 3600 hotel guests (many of them overseas visitors) had to be catered for and the hotel management needed to respond.

Among issues such as access and egress of the guests and hotel supplies, the media were attempting to book rooms overlooking the scene. There had been some damage to windows, hotel staff were traumatised. Communications were confused and mobile phone networks overwhelmed.

In response to the so-called 7/7 bombings, strategic supplies of first aid equipment, blankets etc. are now lodged at critical places such as rail termini.

Because injured and shocked victims had entered nearby premises seeking help, better first aid arrangements and staff training has been implemented against the possibility of further terrorist attacks.

Chapter 5   Major Incident Planning.

Kinds of plans:

A number of plans need to be put in place as part of a DEMS which are always to some extent overlapping, however each stage in a response has its own significant purpose. Note also that some plans cover a short duration and require a very rapid response whereas others need to continue to be implemented for a prolonged timescale, perhaps weeks or months, even years.

TYPE of PLAN	PURPOSE
CONTINGENCY PLAN	To identify the range of worst-case scenarios that may affect the organization. Thereafter to identify the appropriate actions and responses needed (contingencies) to cope with such eventualities. 'Crystal Ball Gazing'
EMERGENCY PLAN (COMAH – NON-COMAH)	Targeted & specific – what actually to do when emergency is declared. It is usually generic and provides the competencies and systems to deal with any kind of event. COMAH plans are specific and need to address the bespoke issues for the site, both onsite and offsite
CRISIS PLAN	More corporate in nature and look at how the organization needs to react It deals with a range of crisis situations which are not just safety related but could be IT, financial, HR, Production etc.
DISASTER RECOVERY PLAN	Actions needed immediately following or during a disaster
BUSINESS CONTINUITY PLAN	A broader plan to ensure that the organization can continue to function beyond the aftermath and into long-term viability.

Phases of response to an emergency

The diagram below illustrates how the 'Blue Light' Category One services and the overlapping involvement of Category Two responses may occur in the immediate aftermath of major incident. Your enterprise should have its own planning which spans these stages and extends beyond into the realm of crisis management and business continuity management.

Importantly: somebody has to be empowered to make the decision to declare an emergency.

Phases in Recovering from an Incident

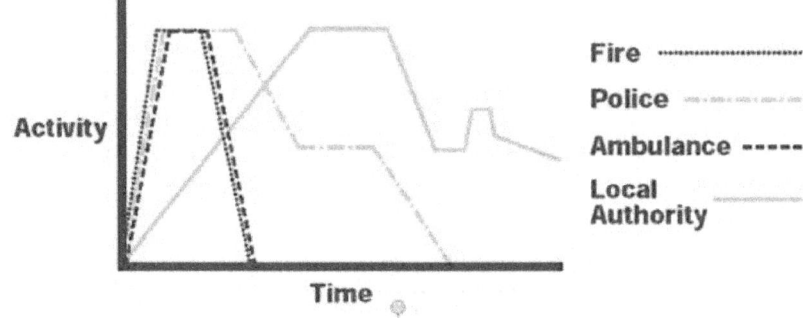

The chart above illustrates the activity of the police, fire and ambulance services and the Local Authority in a 'typical' major incident. Whereas fire and ambulance services have high activity over a short period of time, police involvement will be more protracted, particularly where a crime has been committed.

Source: *Recovery: An Emergency Management Guide (UK Home Office 2006)*

Contingency Planning

Such planning is basically a risk assessment which looks at the various threats to which an organisation may be at risk. Clearly, some threats are more serious than others and so the damage which may occur if they are realised will accordingly have a range of 'worst case scenarios' associated with them, requiring a proportionate management response which must be predetermined. How threat assessment is done falls within the steps in implementing a DEMS.

Recovering from a disaster

Restoring essential services
Cleaning up and restoring
Reconstructing
Assessing economic impact
Maintaining confidence and morale
Catering for welfare needs
Returning to normality as far as possible
Adapting to new realities
Reviewing performance and plans

Recovery management encompasses the physical, social, psychological, political and financial consequences of an emergency.

Anticipation of consequences and appropriate recovery planning must start right from the beginning of any response. Organisations and communities need to plan, manage and undertake those activities that will provide as rapid a return to normality as possible - for both the community and responders.

Lessons from the past emphasise the need to involve the organisation fully in its own recovery. The promotion and support of self-help activities are important considerations.

Involving the organisation fully in its own recovery

Disaster Recovery Planning

Your enterprise will have assets which are vital to your recovery and the plan should detail how these may be recovered or losses minimised.

When Windsor Castle caught fire the many valuable artefacts within the buildings were physically carried to safety by the castle staff. Objects were cleared in a structured manner based on their value, imminence of risk from the fire and ease of removal. As a result of having a proper structured salvage plan, everything except those in the seat of the fire were safely recovered, logged and tagged before removal to a storage repository.

Recovery should start by considering personnel. Persons may be missing, unaccounted for, stranded somewhere or out of contact. Depending on the nature of the disaster they may be injured, perhaps traumatised. The first stage of recovery is establishing a functional team and making arrangements to cover the care of everybody, including families and next of kin, also extending to visitors and other involved third parties. In general three categories of persons should be considered:

Vulnerable persons

Others in the community – including survivors and the bereaved

Responders.

Important physical resources, tools, prototypes, jigs and fixtures, machinery and equipment may be destroyed, damaged lost or impounded (especially if the scene is a crime scene). 'Not having all your eggs in one basket' makes you more resilient. It could be useful to consider where alternative premises could be rented at short notice.

Electronic data storage is pretty well essential nowadays. Data security, often confidential or otherwise critical must be appropriately backed up. Systems should be secure to appropriate standards such as ISO 27001:2013. Follow the hyperlink to the British Standards Institute for details.

http://www.bsigroup.co.uk/en-GB/iso-27001-information-security/ISOIEC-27001-Revision

Vital records may also be held as blueprints, microfiches or plain old paper documents which may be difficult or impossible to recover. It is prudent to make scanned copies of anything important. You might consider firesafe document storage.

Financial valuable assets should also be considered if it is reasonably practicable to salvage them. It is worth considering a rating system so that those carrying out salvage can do so in a planned manner as in the Windsor Castle example (above).

Maintaining the Infrastructure.

As an early stage of business continuity and ongoing with salvage operations, putting assets back into use must be considered. Buildings may need to be assessed for safety, services could need to be checked and verified and access and egress rearranged.

Case Study – the Hospital

A major teaching hospital suffered a serious fire which moved rapidly to the roof then broke through poorly installed fire compartmentation, spreading widely. By the time the fire was extinguished, several areas of the hospital were closed off as unsafe and debris was hanging off the roof over a central courtyard. The first actions were to get surveyors in to make an initial assessment of the building while a mutual aid scheme was activated to refer outpatients to nearby hospitals where (for example) scans and X-Rays could be done.

By the next morning the cleanup had progressed to the point where some wards were reopened along with the operating theatres and some diagnostics. Access and egress, fire escape routes etc. had all to be reassessed in accordance with the Regulatory Reform (Fire Safety) Order 2005.

The hospital had immediate access to financial resource of £3 million and close liason with the insurers to cover emergency costs.

Although the rebuild continued for two years, the hospital was able to function almost normally and certainly so within a week of the fire.

Liason with clients

You will need to consider at an early stage what effect your emergency could have on your client, suppliers and customers. Business interruption is often acceptable for a short while but others in the supply chain have their own priorities. Whilst people are usually sympathetic, once they are forced to seek alternative suppliers, you may lose the business altogether.

Communications

In any emergency it is likely that communications will be centrally and crucially important. Some systems may be disabled or overloaded and there is a dearth of information, especially in the early stages. Later on the reverse may apply so that there is a risk of the response team becoming overwhelmed. In all circumstances it is important that communications are managed so that all the functions of the information cycle (below) are properly controlled. Dependant on the size of the organisation there should be a designated person or a team whose task is to collate and analyse information before passing it on to the decision makers.

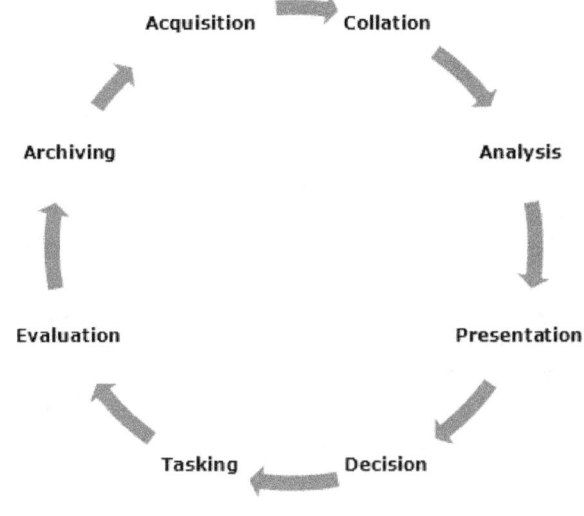

The Information Cycle

During an emergency it is an important task to keep an activity log and this may fall naturally to the communications gathering function. The incident log has many uses in assisting control of an emergency situation, from keeping a check on actions taken by the incident controllers through to being the primary source for debriefing. It may be used as evidence if there are subsequent legal proceedings.

Chapter 6 – Examples of Procedures

Bomb threats

"There's a bomb in the library!"

The university has six libraries on 5 different sites. In the absence of any procedures or protocols a frantic round of phone calls eventually achieved the evacuation of all six about 2 ½ hours later. Following searches by terrified librarians assisted by the police the incident was declared to be a hoax. The perpetrator was never found.

"There's a bomb in the school!"

The warning was telephoned to the switchboard at lunch time on a rainy winter's day. The Headmaster responded by treating it as for a fire evacuation and soon had a thousand children lined up at the fire assembly point opposite the main hall. Some of the younger boys had been playing a supervised game of football and they were also brought to the assembly point, soaking wet and dressed in shorts and singlets.
Police and Fire Brigade attended and advised the Head that it was their responsibility to have the premises searched!
The whole school population had to stand in the cold rain for three quarters of an hour while for many of them their midday meal congealed on the plate. The erstwhile footballers soon began shivering and at risk of becoming hypothermic. Members of staff took off their own coats to help keep them warm and became soaked themselves.
Meanwhile the senior management team were faced with a search involving a thousand bags and satchels!
The search, perfunctory though it was took several (volunteer) members of staff with police assistance the better part of an hour to complete. As most children were bussed in from a neighbouring village it was impractical to close early and everybody spent a wet, miserable afternoon in their classrooms.
The perpetrator was never officially identified but a pupil who had truanted that day was admitted to hospital at the weekend having been severely beaten by a gang of his fellow pupils.

A bomb threat is always a very serious matter and cannot be lightly dismissed, however, a proportionate response can greatly minimise the kind of disruption exemplified above. It is always a criminal act and the police should always be notified.
Having made that point, the vast majority of bomb threats are hoaxes, sometimes malicious against the target organisation, sometimes not, the latter being against society at large. Genuine threats are usually telephoned to the police using codewords. This was extensively done by the IRA during 'The Troubles' in Northern Ireland.

A bomb threat procedure is nothing like a fire evacuation and needs a separate risk assessment (in the UK this is required under the Management of Health & Safety regulations).
Your threat assessment should make a realistic appraisal of the likelihood (typically schools, local authorities) and severity (typically pharmaceutical companies, religious gatherings).

Switchboard operators should have a procedure to work to:

There should be a bomb threat checklist.
Record the conversation as soon as it is realised as a bomb alert.
Try to keep the caller talking and, if possible get an emergency call to the police.
Try to get details ("Whereabouts have you put it?") to assist in narrowing any subsequent search and evacuation.
Do not hang up the phone.

Judgement is required as to whether to evacuate. A device could be placed outside near the fire assembly point or in a public area of the building or on a travel route. It may be safer for persons to remain within the building. Effective management requires intelligent appraisal and invocation of preplanned emergency procedures.

Excellent and detailed advice is available to enable you to devise effective and proportionate response, e.g.
http://www.aaets.org/article99.htm
http://directorate.southwales.ac.uk/media/files/documents/2011-02-15/app_AA.pdf
http://m.fema.gov/explosions

Suspect packages.

An explosive or otherwise dangerous package (containing noxious or infectious substances) can vary from a letter to a holdall and present a concomitant wide variation in hazard. All suspect packages should immediately be reported. Other persons should be warned to leave the area.

A package should NEVER be touched or disturbed in any way.
Nothing electrical should be switched on or off lest it trigger the device.
Doors should be left open to give a clear view for the investigators.

There should be a mail handling system where packages can be scanned. Where an individual is in the public eye (TV personalities, Ministers, company executives etc.) should have all mail inspected as a routine.
http://www.abdn.ac.uk/safety/uploads/files/suspect_packages.pdf

Chapter 7   Media Management

Reputation is one of the most valuable assets your organization has. Normally it takes years to build up but it can be destroyed in a matter of hours or days if, when you face a disaster or emergency, you fail handle it effectively.

Frequently, the public's perception of what has happened and the effectiveness of the response are dictated by the media. The media are the link between your organization and the public.

You should not forget that they are there to do a job, which is to discover and interpret the facts around what, to them, is a story with a headline! It is essential to get them on your side.

You need to have a structured response:

Only one person should deliver press briefings so that there are no contradictions or misunderstandings;

Briefings should be held at appropriately frequent intervals;

It is helpful to find a briefing location where it is calm and quiet so that everyone should be able to hear with clarity and you can answer questions in a considered way free from the immediate stresses of the scenario.

There are some 'golden rules' for media management:

Address your 'real' audience, not the media itself

It is important that, that at a very early stage, an organization identifies its target audience when talking to the media. This may be customers, shareholders, or its staff, the regulatory authority or the general public. Although it may feel like it, it is unlikely to be the media themselves. The media are merely the means by which the message is passed to the wider audience. Having said that, the media are in such a powerful position that they are, in many cases, able to form public opinion and it is necessary to be aware of this.

Acknowledge that there has been a disaster or emergency and be honest.

If it is found that the spokesperson for an organization has told a direct lie or made misleading statements to the media, the disaster or emergency that the company faces will be compounded.

Show concern and be compassionate

Whilst you will be keen to get the business up and running again as quickly as possible, it is vital to show compassion to the people involved, particularly if there have been deaths or injuries. Tony Hayward, BP's CEO and responsible for the 'Deepwater Horizon' disaster infamously remarked that 'I would like to get my life back' – which he did when he was dismissed shortly afterwards!

Be conscious of time

Journalists have deadlines to meet, be it the next television or radio broadcast or the cut-off time to file their reports. Additionally, if the disaster or emergency is regarded as a major news item, television news companies may run it as a 'Breaking News' story, so it is on-screen for lengthy periods.

Be proactive

Not only must you be honest about the facts you must be firm and positive in putting your story across. Where the issues are technical or confusion is likely and you must make the effort to explain them in clear layman's terms. You need to be able to deliver a clearly structured response at the earliest opportunity in order to tell your organization's side of the story. Remember that if you don't, the media will make it up for themselves! There's nothing so potentially destructive as the rumour mill once it gets rolling!

Identify the right spokesperson

I cannot overstate how important it is that you should have a media plan and that should identify who your spokesperson will be. If at all possible, he or she should not be part of the team managing the response. If your organization is involved in technical processes, it may also be necessary to appoint and train people as advisors who have an intimate knowledge of the processes involved.

In addition to being comfortable addressing the media; they should have the skills to develop an empathy and sympathy as to how the media operates and what its requirements are. Specialist media training is available from 'Media Friendly'. They have an excellent website and can give advice and guidance on all aspects of media management planning and training.

http://www.mediafriendly.org/uk-crisis-media-management

'8 Phases to a Crisis: Crisis Life Cycle'

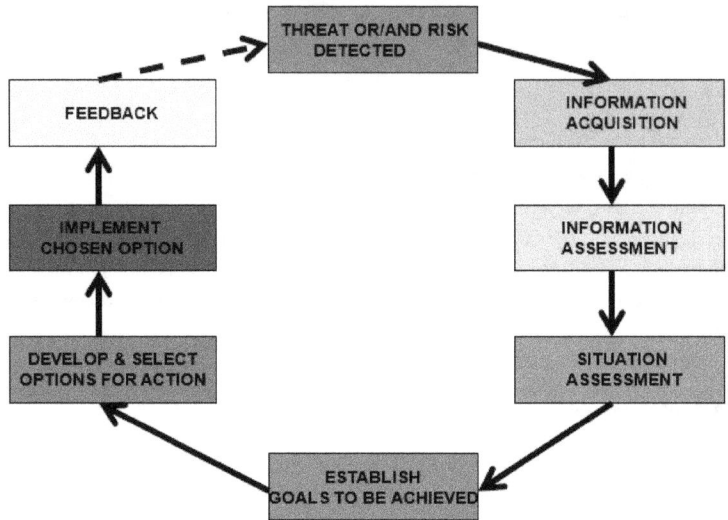

A crisis can onset rapidly (as in the destruction of a key facility) or slowly (as for an epidemic disease) and there are a range of crises, some predictable – and therefore which can be planned for specifically and some not, arising 'out of the blue'. The above model may hopefully give you an insight as to how a crisis may be anticipated, managed and ultimately dealt with.

The cyclic (iterative) structure above is a tool to enable continual improvement in learning how to manage crises. As such it broadly fits in with other management systems and certainly it echoes the DEMS approach of plan-do-check-act.
Once a threat has been recognised as sufficiently serious to be considered to be a potential crisis (and is becoming imminent) then the CMT should be activated.
Recognising the importance of information gathering (see chapter 5 – The Information Cycle) the information management team should be invoked to advise the CMT and enable early assessment so that an initial response can be planned.
Recognising that the CMT provides the leadership role then the outcome needs to be an action plan based on the best option given what is known at the time. You should remember that a crisis is dynamic, serious and requires a robust, proactive response. The option chosen may not be the best one (in the light of hindsight) but often speed of response is often critical. 'He who hesitates is lost' will almost certainly apply!
Once an option has been chosen then the plan can be implemented and mitigation monitored, fed back into the detection and risk assessment phase. As the threat is managed, hopefully it will become reduced by applying control measures until the CMT can be stood down.

Remember that a crisis is something serious, difficult to resolve and threatening to the functioning and survival of your enterprise. It can cover a wide spectrum of possibilities e.g. financial, IT disruption, reputational damage, product recall... and so on.

Crisis Planning

A crisis plan is more holistic and generalised than an emergency or disaster recovery plan. It considers matters in a wider sense and at senior corporate level. It is proactive in prevention or, if that is not possible, then mitigation of the disaster. Its remit extends beyond the essentially reactive emergency planning.

Look at the illustration below and consider ways in which a crisis may occur and so how it can be planned for. As an example, the Buncefield Disaster interrupted the pipeline supply of aviation kerosene to Heathrow Airport and there were insufficient fuel tankers available within the UK to be able to compensate. This in turn meant that aircraft were having to fly with reduced fuel reserves and perforce had to make extra stops, incurring higher costs and route rescheduling and disruption.

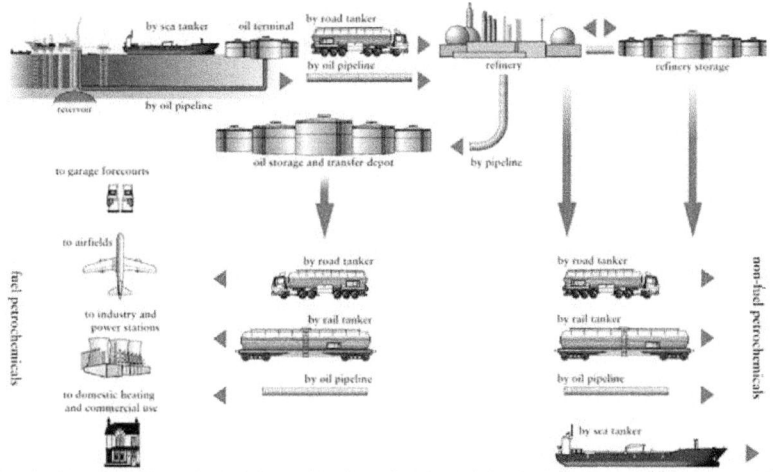

If you look at the above flow diagram, you should be able to identify critical system components and node points where particular vulnerabilities exist.
Gas and oil platforms can be disabled by serious events (fires and explosions, unstoppable oil leaks etc).
Pipelines are particularly vulnerable to supply interruption, sabotage, massive product losses etc.
Lesser incidents such as a strike by tanker drivers, whilst serious, normally do not require the CMT to be activated.

An example of a vulnerable node point was found in a major hospital where all the services ran through a single corridor to the rear of the main complex. A fire involving, say waste collection bins could have disabled the entire hospital!.

In another similar situation, a fire caused by vandalism destroyed three main distribution cables where they all crossed a wooden bridge together causing a widespread power blackout which lasted for several days.

Creating a Crisis Management TEAM (CMT)

4 key participants:

CMT Leader

CMT Coordinator

CMT Communications Representative

CMT Admin & Specialist Support

There needs to be 'CMT A' AND 'CMT B' (shadow and offsite). The CMT is MORE than COMAH On and Off Site Teams. COMAH deals with safety emergencies whilst CMT assesses the broader commercial impact.

The members of the CMT must be top executives, able to make high level decisions and implement them

CMT functions

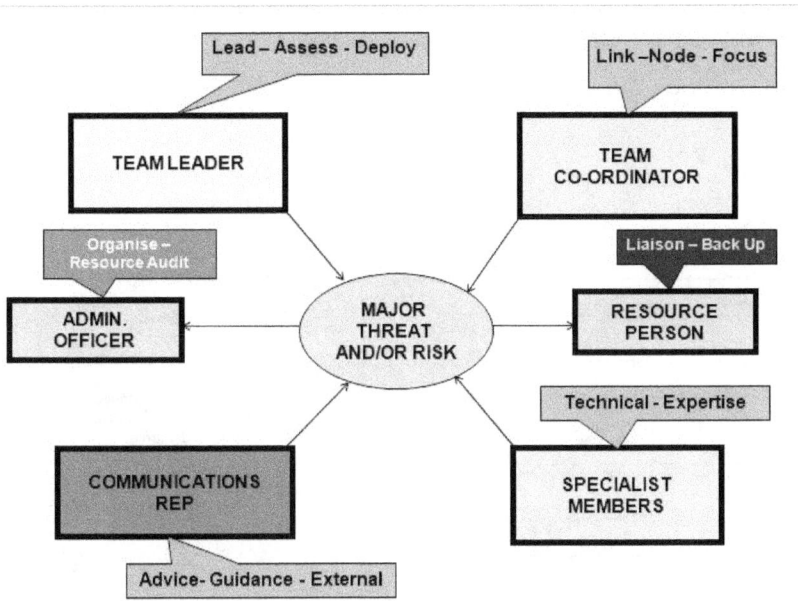

We have already noted the importance of having the right persons with the right skill sets operating at executive level. In setting up this structure it is necessary to identify individuals and preferably duplicate them. Where might you place the leaders, commanders and managers?

Activating the CMT

The CMT is activated if (and only if) there are considered to be 'significant ramifications' arising from the imminent crisis, thus giving structure to the decision taking.

RATING	SAFETY
A CATASTROPHIC	Multiple fatalities of staff, agents and public
B MAJOR	Single fatality of staff, agents or public
C MEDIUM	Serious health impact on multiple members of staff or agents [or one member of public]
D MINOR	Serious impact on one person (staff or agent)
E NEGLIGIBLE	Transient health impact on staff, agents or public

CMT activated if:
-serious harm or death of employees
-serious harm to the environment
-potential financial loss of >£200k
- significant implications as an employer
- adverse media that may arise from the event
- legal or regulatory impact
- significant concerns from key stakeholder groups
- significant and prolonged failure of critical IT systems ?

Chapter 9   Business Continuity (BCM)

Essentially BCM is a strategy for business survival. Specifically this means getting the organisation back into commercial and economic operation as soon as is reasonably practicable following a disaster or emergency. It takes a broader approach than a DEMS although both are strategic in nature.

Business Continuity Management (BCM) is the process of proactively identifying, anticipating, resourcing and planning to ensure that business operations can continue after the Disaster.

Business Continuity Planning (BCP) is a stage in the BCM process. It is the tactical and operational document that will be used when Disaster Strikes.

BCM has its own institute (**the BCI**) and there is an appropriate **ISO 22301:2012** standard.

A good practice guide is available from the BCI http://www.thebci.org

Business Impact Analysis is a risk assessment tool designed to:

Isolate your **key** processes e.g. IT, facilities, finance;

Identify likely threats to each key process;

Give a threat rating to each process;

Prioritise;

Develop control measures ;

Review your actions on a regular basis.

There is also a useful Published Document, *PD 25666:2010 Business continuity management – Guidance on exercising and testing continuity and contingency programmes.*

www.haringey.gov.uk/**business impact assessment** tool.doc

Copy and paste the above link to download a BIA template and planner.

BCM is a phased and reiterative process, a turning wheel of continual improvement.

Understanding your Business: business impact and risk assessment tools are used to identify the critical deliverables and enablers in your business, evaluating recovery priorities and assessing the risks which could lead to business interruption and/or damage to your organisation's reputation.

Continuity Strategies: determining the selection of alternative strategies available to mitigate loss, assessing the relative merits of these against the business environment and their likely effectiveness in maintaining the organisation's critical functions

Exercising &, Plan Maintenance: ongoing plan testing, audit and change management of the Business Continuity Plan and its processes

Developing the Response: improving the risk profile through improvements to operational procedures and practices, implementing alternative business strategies, using risk financing measures (including insurance) and building Business Continuity Plans

Establishing the Continuity Culture: Introduction of the BCM process by education and awareness of all stakeholders, including employees, customers, suppliers and shareholders

Risk ranking can be considered in various ways but here is a scale developed by the Australian National Audit Office

LEVEL OF IMPACT	ASSESSMENT	SCORE
EXTREME	THREATENS POLITICAL & BUSINESS VIABILITY	5
MAJOR	SIGNIFICANT IMPACT ON BUSINESS DRIVERS	4
MODERATE	MAJOR IMPACT ON SHORT TERM BUSINESS OPERATION	3
MINOR	INCONVENIENT BUT NO REAL ONGOING BUSINESS IMPACT	2
NIL	RECONSIDER THE INCLUSION OF THIS AS A CRITICAL RESOURCE	1

Once the risk ranking for significant threats has been established then a strategy can be evolved.

Business Continuity Strategies

Do nothing – in some instances the board may consider the risk commercially acceptable.

Changing or ending the process – deciding to alter existing procedures but must be done bearing in mind the organisation's key focus.

Insurance – provides financial recompense / support in the event of loss, but does not provide protection for brand and reputation.

Loss Mitigation – tangible procedures to eliminate / reduce risk.

Business Continuity Planning : an approach that seeks to improve organisational resilience to interruption, allowing for the recovery of key business and systems processes within the recovery time frame objective, whilst maintaining the organisation's critical functions.

Chapter 10   Stress and trauma response (PTSD)

Pan Am flight 103 – 'The Lockerbie Disaster'

A transatlantic flight from Frankfurt to Detroit via London and New York City that was destroyed by a terrorist bomb on Wednesday, 21 December 1988, killing all 243 passengers and 16 crew on board. Large sections of the aircraft crashed into Lockerbie, Scotland, killing 11 more people on the ground.

We are all individuals and so we all make an individual response to a traumatic event. In the context of DEMS, such an event is likely to be 'one off' and perhaps the more traumatic for that reason. We shouldn't forget, though that our individual responses will be within the larger framework of a workplace and may also involve the wider community. For example, when the Lockerbie disaster occurred and a Boeing 747 passenger aircraft crashed on the town, the community response and its management were vital in enabling the stricken town to recover.

The Local Authority produced a report detailing the community response which stresses the human side of this dreadful event. You should read it.

http://www.dumgal.gov.uk/CHttpHandler.ashx?id=1687&p=0

As individuals we may respond positively or we may be overcome and unable to function. Until it happens to you, you won't really know.

It is different for the professional responders insofar as they are trained and accustomed to deal with traumatic events and they have access to professional support, however they too are vulnerable and it is a duty on their employers under Occupational Safety & Health legislation to carry out appropriate risk assessments (suitable and sufficient) and have a policy to handle occupational stress issues.

Post Traumatic Stress Disorder (PSTD)

Within the wider scope of anxiety disorders PSTD is recognised as a specific condition and has definable symptoms which may have legal significance. PSTD is beyond the 'normal' compass of human response to traumatic events which may vary widely between individuals (summary below).

RESPONSE	DESCRIPTION	
TRAUMA	SHOCK	
STRESS	PRESSURES – DEMANDS-COPING	
DEPRESSION	DESPONDENCY – FEELING LOW	
ANXIETY	UNEASINESS – IRRITABILITY	
PTSD	NEGATIVE AFTERMATH OF TRAUMA – 'LIFE CHAOS'	

To be diagnosed with PTSD, the person must have been exposed to a traumatic event in which both of the following were present:

a)   the person experienced, witnessed, or was confronted with an event or events that involved actual or threatened death or serious injury, or a threat to the physical integrity of self or others; and

b).....the person's response to the trauma involved intense fear, helplessness, or horror. (In children, this may be expressed instead by disorganized or agitated behaviour.)

Stressful events of daily life that do not meet these criteria include divorce and financial crises, which may lead to adjustment problems, but are not sufficient to meet criterion a) for PTSD.

PTSD develops in people who were exposed to traumatic events that involved an actual or perceived threat of death or serious injury to them, their loved ones or significant others. The symptoms develop usually within the first one to three months after the event. Sufferers from PTSD characteristically re-experience aspects of the traumatic event in the form of vivid experiences that the event is recurring (flashbacks), distressing and intrusive images of the event, or nightmares. Reminders of the traumatic event (people, situations or circumstances resembling or associated with the event) often arouse intense distress or physiological reactions. Attempts to avoid such reminders are another characteristic feature of PTSD. Many people develop symptoms of hyperarousal: being excessively vigilant, easily startled, irritable, or having difficulty concentrating and in sleeping. Many PTSD sufferers describe feeling detached from others, unable to experience feelings and losing interest in previously important activities. PTSD may be associated with depression, anxiety, or panic and may lead some to use harmful amounts of alcohol or other addictive substances.

Most survivors of catastrophic events will initially develop symptoms of PTSD of varying intensity, but the vast majority will recover within the following year, or years, without treatment, or with informal support from families and friends. However, up to a third may continue to have distressing symptoms many years after the event.

Source: http://www.thecochranelibrary.com/details/collection/1045825/Cochrane-Evidence-Aid-resources-for-post-traumatic-stress-disorder-following-nat.html

So it is complicated and requires psychiatric assessment. It also needs to be taken seriously.

Psychological disorders are to be expected following trauma and require a managed response at the earliest possible stage.

Factors present in the acute-phase recovery environment of a disaster have been found to aggravate stress reactions and therefore increase survivors' risk of developing negative outcomes (Emergency Management Australia, 1999) (*Excerpted from Raphael, Disaster Mental Health Response Handbook, NSW Health, 2000*). These include:

Lack of emotional and social support

Presence of other stressors such as fatigue, cold, hunger, fear, uncertainty, loss, dislocation, and other psychologically stressful experiences

difficulties at the scene

lack of information about the nature and reasons for the event

lack of, or interference with, self-determination and self-management; treatment in an authoritarian or impersonal manner

lack of follow-up support in the weeks following the exposure.

There is always a need for proactive management of stress-linked disorders. The Stress Management Standards (UK HSE) make a good starting point and are available online along with other stress guidance.

http://www.hse.gov.uk/stress/standards

Any significant organisation should in any case have a stress policy within its Health & Safety Policy with guidelines for implementation.

The linkage to the DEMS is via this policy to be implemented following traumatic exposures. Counselling is invariably an early step along with medical referral for individuals having difficulties in readjusting.

Chapter 11   Steps in a DEMS

So far I have been setting the scene and hopefully will have convinced you, the reader, of the importance of having a DEMS in place. The very survival of your enterprise and maybe that of those who work for you and with you, possibly your own survival could depend on it. So how to go about it?

The first stage, hopefully has been reached already because you are reading this and therefore are aware of the need. Your personal commitment is essential and you will need to convince everybody with executive powers because everybody will have a role to play.

Establishing a DEMS methodology

Companies have numerous policies and it is essential that the DEMS policy is compatible with them. You will appreciate that DEMS is an overarching, top level (Board Level) policy. This book recommends that you use the Deming Cycle (plan, do, check, act) as a management template.

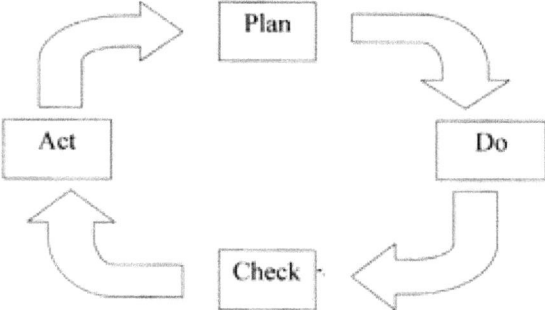

This structure fits well with other management systems which you may already have implemented e.g.:

BS OHSAS 18001:2007 Occupational health and safety management systems- Requirements;
BS EN ISO 9001:2000 Quality Management Systems;
BS EN ISO 14001:2014 Environmental Management Systems;
BS ISO/IEC 27001:2013 Information Security Management Systems;
BS ISO/IEC 20000-2:2012 IT Service Management.

Adapting the template to the specifics of DEMS looks like this:

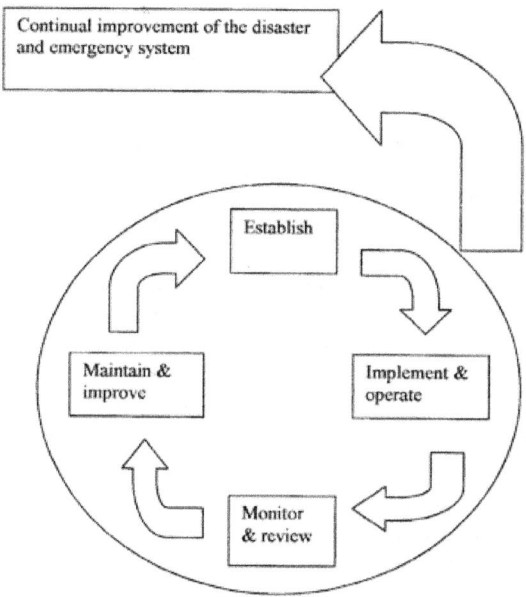

Plan	**Establish** DEMS policy, objectives, targets, controls, processes and procedures relevant to managing risk and improving DEMS to deliver results in accordance with the organization's overall policies and objectives
Do	**Implement and operate** the DEMS policy, controls, processes and procedures
Check	**Monitor and review** performance against DEMS objectives and policy, report results to management for review, and determine, and authorise actions for remediation and improvement
Act	**Maintain and improve** the DEMS by taking preventive and corrective actions, based on the results of the management review and re-appraising the scope of the DEMS policy and objectives

Writing a DEMS policy

The policy statement is effectively your mission statement. It should be specific and targeted to the activities of your enterprise and signed by the most senior director. The policy applies to all levels of management and all premises owned or operated by it. It should be reviewed on a regular basis, usually annually.

It should include the following sections:

 a commitment to the prevention of harm to all employees, contractors, clients, customers, suppliers, harm to the social environment, damage to physical assets, and to the physical environment, and in addition to ensure business continuity;

a commitment to comply with the legal framework within which the organisation operates that relate to its DEMS;

to make suitable, proactive and efficient arrangements to cope with any disaster or emergency should it occur, this includes the commitment of human, physical and financial resources to undertake the necessary activities required at each phase of the disaster or emergency, and with respect to business continuity;

to consult with all parties likely to be affected by any adverse incident;

is documented, implemented and maintained;

is communicated to all persons working under the control of the organization with the intent that they are made aware of their individual DEMS obligations;

is made available to all interested parties; and

is reviewed periodically to ensure that it remains relevant and appropriate.

> Signed, dated and displayed as appropriate

Threat assessment

At an early stage in setting up your DEMS you will need to carry out a threat assessment. You should remember the definition of threat as being an event that has the potential to destroy or severely damage your enterprise.

Generic threats.

These are the kinds of event which can impact upon us all to a greater or lesser degree, though you need to look at them in the context of your own enterprise.

National Risk Register: An illustration of the high consequence risks facing the UK

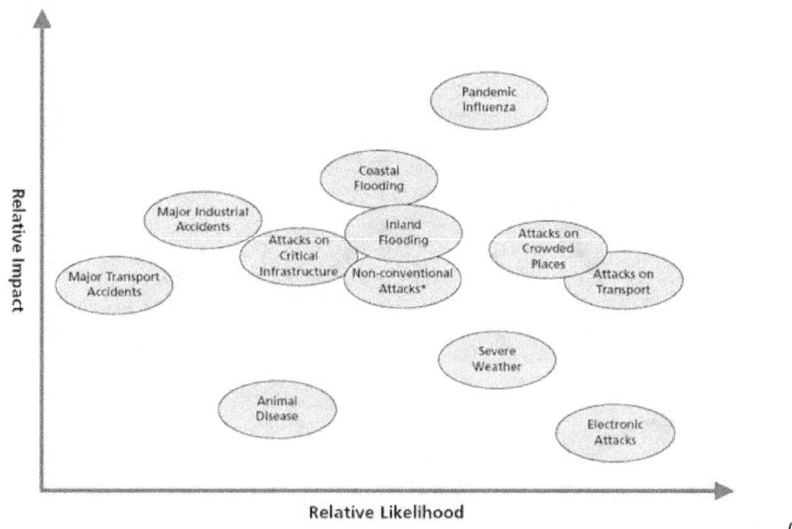

. (Source UK Cabinet Office, Civil Contingencies Secretariat).

(They don't use the word threat but that is what they mean!)

Relative Impact of threats.

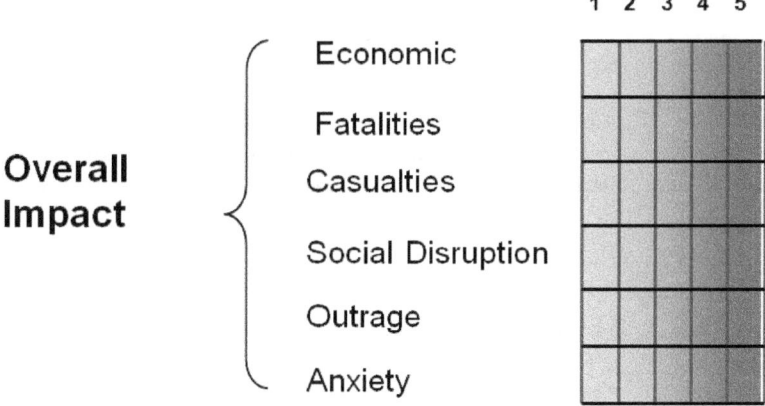

These impacts can be graded according to their severity and you will need to evaluate their significance to your own enterprise, for example if your premises are on a hilltop then you don't have a high flood risk but every organisation is to some extent disrupted by an influenza pandemic, both directly (staff incapacitated), and indirectly (infrastructure disruption).

Assessment of Likelihood.

Traditional risk assessment of likelihood or probability of an occurrence is based on the number of events over time using statistical methods, typically accident incidence rates. RIDDOR is one such source. When it comes to threats then the occurrences are (thankfully!) low, albeit the consequences are often very severe and a different approach is needed.

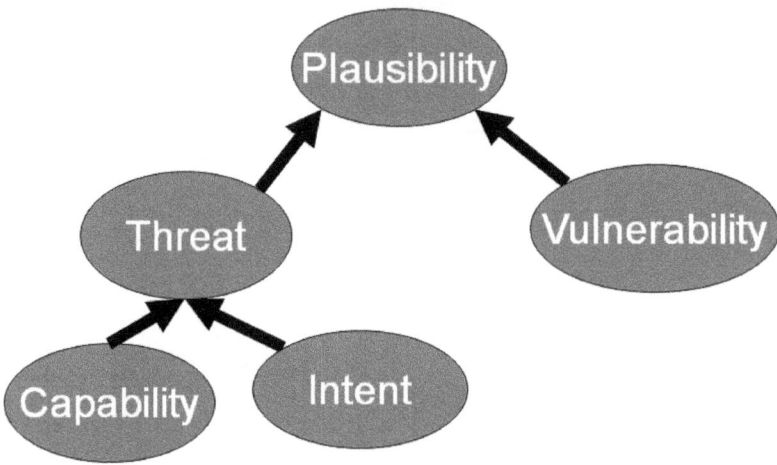

Threat assessment and vulnerability.

The above diagram indicates how viable threats are linked to weaknesses in an organisation's systems which makes it vulnerable and the threat scenario to become plausible. Threat alert levels are based on this approach, matching security response to perceived threat levels (low – medium – high) obtained from intelligence or incidents which have occurred. Whilst this model is particularly applicable to terrorism threats it can be used in a more general sense.

Likelihood, and severity – threat matrix

We can arrive at a risk assessment matrix by combining severity and probability in the same way as we do for health & safety risk assessments except that the paradigm shifts upwards, the stakes are much higher!

A DEMS risk assessment is only needed for such threats as are considered to be significant to the organisation as a whole. Lesser threats (hazards) should be managed as health & safety risks.

As with all risk assessment, DEMS threat assessment requires a degree of judgement.

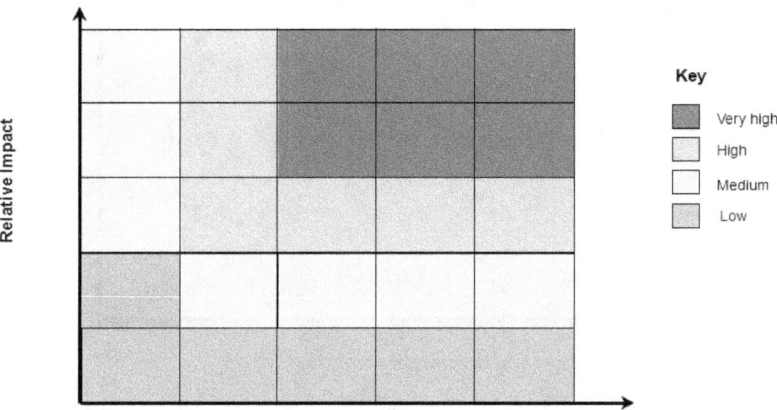

Relative Likelihood

Key
■ Very high
□ High
□ Medium
▨ Low

Identifying and ranking threats

We have already seen the UK Cabinet Office generic threats and an indication of their likelihood. Threat assessment is essentially a dynamic risk assessment process which can change as new experiences or new intelligences are gained. The impact versus likelihood matrix was drawn up before the winter of 2014 produced massive flooding throughout the UK so the likelihood of flooding will now be ranked higher than shown here.

Specific Threats.

In planning your DEMS, you will need to draw up a list of specific threats to your enterprise and rank their likelihood. They can then be inserted into a semi-quantitative grid or matrix as above, the output being an overall risk ranking. Specific threats will depend very much on the occupational sector so that for a chemical plant, for example the emphasis will be on the consequences of plant failure and any major plant will be subject to COMAH planning. In contrast a company running care homes for the elderly could have reputational issues, fire risk and food poisoning as high on their risk ranking.

A logical approach to threat identification as illustrated below will assist in creating a coherent listing.

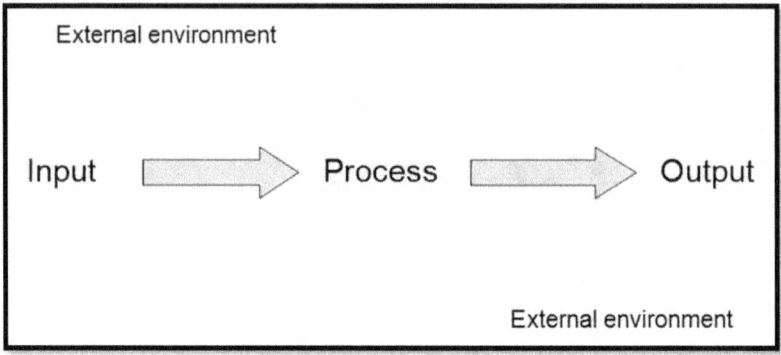

History of accidents within an industry, Isomorphic learning.

Virtually every industry or enterprise has a history of past accidents and often it seems to be the case that such scenarios repeat themselves and often for the same underlying reasons. It is an aspect of DEMS to bring past histories within the threat matrix and learn from them.

Unpredictable threats.

Many threats fall into this category so the risk assessment process cannot be applied to them. For this reason DEMS concerns itself with generic controls to mitigate harm, assist recovery and minimise business disruption.

Horizon scanning.

As a part of the monitoring process it should be a management activity to anticipate and observe distant events. For example an outbreak of Ebola Virus infections occurred in central Africa towards the end of March 2014 and has reached as far as Canada by August 2014. A timely reminder, then that H1N1 so called 'avian 'flu' pandemic can arise at any time and will surely affect all of us to some extent.

Political instabilities (currently Russian annexation of the Crimea) and the tragedies unfolding in Syria and Gaza mean increased terrorism alert levels worldwide.

Putting controls in place

Once you have drawn up a register of foreseeable threats and ranked them then you can draw up appropriate control measures in order to manage them. As an example, making provision for firefighting runoff water by collecting it in a lagoon for treatment and disposal controls the threat of prosecution and swingeing fines and cleanup costs (£1.3 million for breach of the Water Resources Act 1991).

Management may involve physical resource such as improved security (a good example is increased measures to prevent arson (deliberate firesetting), such as are advised by the Fire Protection Association https://www.thefpa.co.uk/fpa_home). Management may simply involve drawing up a list of actions to be taken if a threat is realised. Examples here could concern employees working overseas where there is a risk of kidnapping or danger to life from political instability.

Controlling unforeseeable threats.

Crucial to the effective operation of a DEMS is the ability to respond in a resilient way to whatever may arise and this involves both leadership and management within your organisation. A leader, director, makes the decisions as an event unfolds. Leaders need to be trained in that role. A leader needs to be able to respond in stressful circumstances in real-time and with often limited information available. The outcome of the leader's decisions may literally have life and death consequences.

Management is different. The managers should be able to implement plans and procedures in a competent and structured way, albeit in rapidly changing circumstances and in varying operational levels. A Gold Commander is basically the leader, Silver Commander is the top layer of manager and Bronze level command involves front-line operations, implementation of procedures and systems.

An effective DEMS ensures that an event is mitigated with the participants acting as a coordinated team.

Building organisational resilience.

When disaster strikes it may be at any time or at any place or places within an organisation. It is of primary importance that communications operate effectively so that contact details and availability of key persons is assured. In a serious emergency the normal media may be temporarily out of action. Mobile phone networks may become overloaded and break down. The internet may fail. Landlines are more reliable but can also be compromised. Local radio stations could prove useful and sometimes national television and radio can relay information.

As an example of this, a plume of asbestos containing material was released from a fire in Southeast London, blowing for perhaps 10km over the suburbs. The BBC put out advice over the evening news as to how householders should respond, closing doors and windows, gathering up the material, bagging it and leaving it for a specially organised waste collection. This action undoubtedly minimised asbestos exposure to the populace and proved to be an excellent mitigation of the incident.

The police assume overall control of a major incident so that they can be used to relay critical information and even bring key persons to the scene.

Plan:

Establish the policy, integrate it with other existing policies such as health & safety and environmental management;
Devise a command and control structure and organise communications;
Decide who will be authorised to declare the emergency and thus initiate the emergency plan;
Create a threat list and grade in accordance with seriousness of outcome;
List, with location details the assets which may be available and make preplanned links with suppliers of critical equipment;
Write specific procedures for responding to listed specific threats.

Do:

Implement and operate policy, control process & procedures.

This is the organisation and arrangements section of the DEMS policy. This is where you decide who does what and how that is to be carried out.

Start with the existing organisation chart and assign roles to those persons (or job descriptions) within it. Job descriptions will need to be extended to encompass extra responsibilities.

It will require consultation throughout your organisation. Individual discussion, department meetings, union meetings, safety committee meetings are all good places for this and will raise awareness and hopefully buy in commitment by your colleagues.

Training is critically important if employees are to be able to operate the operating procedures that need to have been written and modified in the light of experience.

Procedures and systems should be 'smart', that wonderful management acronism which is now somewhat of a mantra but important if they should work properly. Overly complex and unworkable procedures have often been cited as factors in failing to do what needs to be done!

'S'   specific

'M'   measurable

'A'   achievable

'R'   realistic

'T'   time bound

Equipment should be sourced as required, for example backups for critical functions, located as appropriate, labelled up and kept properly stocked so that it is available at short notice. Inventories should be recorded with location, content and purpose and be maintained (think of fire extinguishers and you have it!)

Procedures should be trialled and modified as necessary and this should be an iterative process so that you achieve continual improvement.

Check:

Monitor and review against objectives and targets.

Any management system should set objectives and targets so that there is something specific to monitor against. Dated and comprehensive records should be kept of all aspects of the system (think of a fire logbook as an example).

Training and exercising will help to keep the DEMS live and functioning, maintaining readiness should it ever become necessary to implement it.

Act:

Maintain, making improvements and taking preventive and corrective action.

Exercising has been proven to be the most single important management aspect in operating a successful DEMS. Desktop exercises, system tests, live exercising should all be regularly carried out, logged and reviewed. (think of fire drills, extinguisher inspections, alarm tests).

The system should be monitored, much as with any other management activity and regularly reviewed. Debriefing is especially important following exercising or a real incident or near-miss occurrence.

Continually improve: feedback review and audit outcomes into the policy.

Chapter 12   Conclusions

Applying DEMS theory to your organisation

No matter how large or small your enterprise may be, it should have a DEMS, essentially driven at Board level. In its absence the company may fail to anticipate, prevent or mitigate and ultimately survive an emergency. This then could turn into a disaster!

Even if you have a DEMS, it is only as good as the commitment given to it and the appropriateness of the DEMS policy. Moreover, if it is not practiced, kept up to date and reviewed from time to time, the company may yet fail.

Thus it is a key responsibility of the company's executive but at the same time, it should be structured in a proportionate way so that does not become needlessly cumbersome or otherwise ineffective and fail to operate when it is needed.

The example given below which happened to a medium sized enterprise illustrates the value of having a DEMS.

Case Study – the foundry.

The foundry made aluminium and ferrous castings, operating from a mature site which had expanded somewhat haphazardly up to its physical limits. The safety advisor was interested in promoting a DEMS and called in a consultant to assist with an initial status review. The consultant helped to set up the policy along with an environmental policy, a compliance assessment and the development of an aspect register. He was concerned particularly at the environmental risk exposure due to the large amount of materials, especially liquid chemicals stored on site and suggested a review – and that a drains plan be obtained. (This constituted a predictable threat of moderate severity and high likelihood.)

One week later, a tanker driver arrived to deliver a consignment of flammable resin used in the sand casting process. He was told to deliver into one of two tanks and, due to lack of supervision, began to discharge into the wrong one which, alas, was not bunded. Shortly after pumping began, the tank overflowed and then failed catastrophically, dumping 20,000 litres of the resin into the yard.

Due to fire risk, the Fire Brigade were asked to attend, they followed procedure and called in the local Environment Agency officer. On attendance, his first act was to ask for a site drainage plan (which had been obtained only two days before!). The safety advisor instructed the maintenance team to shovel casting sand into the drains and organised the tanker driver to begin recovery using a low-level strainer. As a result the foundry management were commended for their prompt and efficient emergency response. During the incident, the local newspaper phoned in and the Safety Advisor was able to tell them that, yes, they had had an environmental emergency but that the EA had commended them for the effective operation of their emergency plan!

The 20,000 litre tank was written off but in the meantime production resumed from two IBCs (Intermediate Bulk Containers), a tenfold reduction of inventory, and this arrangement became permanent.

The safety advisor was promoted.

This case has most of the elements of a successful DEMS implementation, albeit on a small scale (although highly significant for the foundry's executive).

Crucially, the Safety Advisor showed true leadership qualities. Although he was only appointed to make improvements to the company's Health & Safety policy, he had the vision to appreciate the need for both DEMS and an Environmental Management System and go about implementing them. When the emergency happened, his initial response was to call in the fire brigade to deal with the risk of a serious fire which could easily have destroyed the entire works. Once that was covered he modified the emergency plan to manage the serious risk of pollution of controlled waters, including groundwater and concomitant fines and cleanup costs under the Water Resources Act 1991.

A Standard Operating Procedure for dealing with spillages was invoked and successfully controlled this major product release, most of it being returned to the tanker for shipping back to the supplier.

Acting for the Board as the most senior person then onsite he needed to liase with the emergency services, the regulator and the local media.
His promotion was well deserved!

Appropriateness to size and type of organisation.

Your DEMS should reflect the scope of the organisation. The issues you need to plan for should be appropriate to the industry or commercial sector you operate in. The obvious starting point is any other management systems you have in place and especially Business Continuity. If you haven't a BCM strategy in place then you should consider its development as a co-strategy with DEMS as they have many themes in common.

Quality Management, Health & Safety, Environmental Management, perhaps also Security Management and Premises Management are all systems which you should have in place and which will shape and inform the DEMS you create. For example, if you operate in the food sector then quality and food safety management via HACCP will be dominant factors. If you are a school then security and safety, premises management will come high on the list.

Case Study – the pre-school

The privately operated pre-school took in children ranging from 2.5 to 5 years from a suburban catchment. There were about 250 on the register and a staff of mostly part-time employees.

An outbreak of gastrointestinal disorders broke out in the district, involving children from the school as well as others in the community. The Environmental Health Department decided to close the school canteen down and quarantine it pending further investigations. This action closed the school overnight so that the school management had to turn away the parents at the gate next morning, many of whom were working mothers. The disruption was considerable.

At this stage the school enjoyed a good reputation and a good working relationship with the parents and so this first shock was managed without rancour.

The school had a workable emergency plan which was invoked by the Headmistress as soon as the closure occurred. Although there had been insufficient time in which to pre-notify the parents, the administrative staff had been able to produce an explanatory leaflet and this was handed out when they turned up in the morning plus there was an opportunity to use the staff to explain the predicament.

Although they did not know how long the school would be closed, they could discuss that with parents and promise to phone out to people, send emails and possibly letters as soon as they knew anything as that enabled persons to make alternative temporary arrangements.

The leaflet made a standard apology. It stressed that the closure was as a precaution and that the school may not be the source of the outbreak. It gave out the school telephone number and website, suggesting that parents checked out the latter before telephoning because they had limited capacity to handle calls.

This was the first stage of the disaster recovery plan. The EHO was asked if the school could reopen on a limited basis with children bringing packed lunches and eating in their classrooms and this was agreed provided that extra hygiene precautions were put into place and arrangements for extra food waste disposal. The canteen area remained out of bounds and was, in fact locked up with notices posted. It became necessary to temporarily alter the fire evacuation routes but that was all.

By the third day two-thirds of the children were enabled to return and the school was effectively running to capacity by the following Monday. The canteen was released a week later following a deep clean, however it had not proven to be the source of the outbreak.

Prompt and effective action kept the disruption to a minimum and actually enhanced the school's reputation. There was minimal loss of fee income but no other adverse outcome. If they had not acted effectively in the early stages it was more than likely that some children would have gone to other pre-schools in the area. Good communications with the parents were paramount to the successful resolution of the emergency.

Assessing significant threats.

You will recall that there are both generic and specific threats that may impact on your organisation. Generic threats will tend to affect most enterprises and often at the same time. Thus, for example severe weather may prevent your employees reaching work and your work issues may have knock-on effects to clients or customers and vice-versa. Staffing shortages may limit some of your activities. Importantly, key persons may be unable to attend and may also have communication difficulties. A similar situation would apply in an outbreak of an epidemic.

These and similar threats are best addressed by overall resilience within your organisation. Redundancy (duplication) of systems and shadowing of critical functions (understudying), backup power supplies, callout lists, communication links, financial reserves, holding critical stock levels, working from home, temporary accommodation etc. should all be planned for and built into the DEMS arrangements.

Prevention and mitigation

It is very important to have carried out a thorough threat assessment because this enables the development of plans to manage specific risks and to resource them adequately, having regard to their severity. A good example of such a plan is to have purchased spill kits against the eventuality of an accidental (or sometimes deliberate) release of product. Of course, for successful implementation and mitigation of the potential consequences, there has to be an alert system and a rapid response team who have been adequately trained. Periodic exercising of the plans is considered to be of high importance if they are to function effectively in an emergency and it is worth noting that a staff with raised awareness of such recovery planning will be more overall alert and may identify potential emergencies before they happen.

It is a well-known military dictum that most plans fail when they encounter the enemy. This means that however well an eventuality may have been planned for and rehearsed, we must be prepared for things to go wrong. The concept here is of dynamic risk assessment and it means that team leaders must be just that – leaders!

DEMS concerns itself with systems rather than plans.

Creating a management team and structure

When disaster strikes, it is the leaders who will direct operations. People are not 'born' leaders, they must be trained into the role. Some persons are temperamentally unsuitable to act in a leadership capacity, thus it is important for your organisation to identify who is most fitted to lead, not necessarily the titular head (the managing director or chief executive). The very term 'Managing Director' is confusing in the DEMS context.

There are broadly three functions needed: leadership, command and management. And those placed in these roles must be capable of operating as a team. They will inevitably comprise the crisis management team if the emergency develops in that way.

The DEMS team should be chosen with care, playing to the skills of those you have available within the organisation. In broad terms, the leader equates to 'Gold Commander', the commander to 'Silver' and the managers to 'Bronze'.

Liason with other responders, the media and the public.

In an emergency situation, your organisation will be working with the support of external agencies, the police as overall command and the fire and rescue services as technical command. It is likely that your DEMS team will need to interact with and form part of the overall response, working with responders at these levels and attending meetings. You will be the onsite functionaries and expected to provide site-specific information, coordinate onsite communications and keep the statutory responders appraised of any dangerous developments.

Inevitably there will be liason with other bodies, Category 2 responders and most likely the Local Authority. Maybe also the Environment Agency. Media management has already been discussed.

The value of preplanning and rehearsal cannot be overstated. It is worth considering exercising at various levels and such exercising can range from table-top through to full scale scenarios. The 'blue light' services are generally keen to participate, sharpen their plans and gain familiarity with your operations.

Exercising

There is excellent advice about exercising from the UK government:
https://www.gov.uk/emergency-planning-and-preparedness-exercises-and-training

The Case Study which follows will hopefully give you ideas as to how to create your own bespoke one. If nothing else it was fun and a learning experience for the participants

Case Study – The train crash exercise.

A local authority ran a live exercise in consideration of its duties as a Category Two responder. Approx. 100 members of the public volunteered to participate. The scenario was that these were persons involved who were uninjured survivors passed back from the forward casualty clearing station and transferred in minibuses to the civic centre.

Each person had their own pseudonym and script to work to. Two persons had head injuries, one with a large plaster over one eye, the other had been given no medical support. Some persons had urgent need to be elsewhere, for example to collect children from school. One had an important business meeting in Brussels and needed onward transportation via Eurostar. Some persons had lost contact with (presumed injured or missing) family members. Most persons did not have any personal belongings with them including mobile phones, money/ credit cards and car keys.

The LA staff were volunteers or had been told off to participate and had little training in dealing with shocked and disoriented persons, certainly in such large numbers.

Refreshments were provided in the form of tea and biscuits and were adequate for the situation. Groups of five persons were selected for 'clerking in' and initial counselling at five desk stations. The LA officials had to complete a form giving details of the persons and making arrangements to despatch them on to other transportation or simply to leave and make their own way.

The process was far too slow. Two members of staff circulated amongst the large group in order to answer questions and attempt to prioritise handling. Occasional briefings were given regarding the rescue and recovery.

People began to share stories. Some had mobiles and were usually generous in allowing others to use them to call family, friends or work colleagues.

The two concussed individuals were identified by other persons who conversed with them and noticed that they were unwell. These were referred on to a doctor who was in attendance.

It became clear that communication was a critical need and the importance of attempting to recover personal belongings from the scene of the accident. The LA did not have enough phones to satisfy the needs of those now waiting.

It was only when an individual had been processed and discharged that they encountered a desk set up by a specialist charity who attended such incidents with a remit to help with communications, order taxis, make arrangements with family members to collect them etc.

The debrief concluded that whilst the recovery operation was basically successful, it had been inefficient, especially in processing persons and in communications generally. The underuse of the specialist charity was a particular failure and was due in part to the fact that they turned up uninvited!

Some good suggestions emerged and especially in circulating a proforma to the waiting persons so as to speed up the whole process.

Another exercise is now planned to build on the success of this one.

Maximising resilience.

And finally, resilience is what it is all about. If your organisation has a DEMS in place and the emergency happens, you have a vastly better chance of riding it out, perhaps emerging with an enhanced reputation. You have nothing to lose but the work in setting up DEMS and you have everything to gain at a company, professional and personal level.

Good Luck and good wishes!

Professional Bodies

ICPEM. The Institute of Civil Protection and Emergency Management.

http://www.icpem.net

IIRSM. The International Institute of Risk and Safety Management.

http://www.iirsm.org

Emergency Planning Society.

https://www.the-eps.org

FPA. The Fire Protection Association.

https://www.thefpa.co.uk/fpa_home

EPC. Emergency Planning College

http://www.epcollege.com

BCI. Business Continuity Institute

http://www.thebci.org

BSI. British Standards Institute

http://www.bsigroup.com

List of Acronyms.

ACOP	Approved Code of Practice
ACPO	Association of Chief Police Officers
ANAO	Australian National Audit Office
BCI	Business Continuity Institute
BCM	Business Continuity Management
BIA	Business Impact Analysis
BSI	British Standards Institute
CA	Competent Authority
CaCFOA	Chief & Assistant Chief Fire Officers Association
CBA	Cost - Benefit Analysis
CEO	Chief Executive Officer
CMT	Crisis Management Team
COMAH	Control of Major Accident Hazards
COP	Code of Practice
DEMC	Disaster & Emergency Cycle
DEMS	Disaster and Emergency Management System
EA	Environment Agency
EHO	Environmental Health Officer
EMS	Environmental Management System
EPC	Emergency Planning college
EPS	Emergency Planning society
FEMA	Federal Emergency Management Agency (USA)
HACCP	Hazard Analysis and Critical control Points
HSE	Health and Safety Executive
ICPEM	Institute of Civil Protection & Emergency Planning
IFSEC	International Fire & Security Exhibition & conference
IIRSM	International Institute of Risk & Safety Management
ILO	International Labour Organisation
ISO	International Organisation for Standardisation
IT	Information Technology
MAPP	Major Accident Prevention Policy
OHSAS	Occupational Health and Safety Assessment Series
PIO	Police Incident Officer
PTSD	Post Traumatic Stress Disorder
RPG	Risk Planning Group
RRF	Regional Resilience Forum
SARS	Severe Acute Respiratory Syndrome
UNEP	United Nations Environment Programme
WHO	World Health Organisation

Bibliography

Tolley's Handbook of Disaster and Emergency Management: T Moore & R Lakha

Elsevier Ltd.   ISBN-13:   978-0-75-066990-0

Disaster and Emergency Management Systems: T Moore.
BSI.   ISBN 978-0-580-60710-3

Other titles by the same author

A sister publication 'Managing the Environment' complements this book on Disaster and Emergency Management Systems.

Available as an e-book on Smashwords, Amazon and Kobo.

Also for light relief a Sci-fi ebook entitled:
'Alpha Seven' and
'The Alpha Project – Part One'

Plus as a freebie

'Reject' – a sardonic look at British Industry in the sixties and seventies!